Gift Beyond Measure

Inspiring poems for Christmas

Howard Webber

O&U
Onwards & Upwards

Onwards and Upwards Publishers

4 The Old Smithy
London Road
Rockbeare
EX5 2EA
United Kingdom

www.onwardsandupwards.org

First edition, published in the United Kingdom by Onwards and Upwards Publishers Ltd. (2021).

Illustrations:	Sarah Park
ISBN:	978-1-78815-914-2
Typeface:	Sabon LT

About the Author

Following a career in the NHS as a Medical Laboratory Scientist, during which time he recommitted his life to Jesus, Howard entered training to become a Salvation Army officer/minister, together with his wife Judy. Having been ordained/commissioned, the next 30 years were spent in corps/church leadership and as an itinerant evangelist and corps/church planter.

Howard's first book, *Meeting Jesus – Inspiring stories of modern-day evangelism*, won *Christianity* (now *Premier Christianity*) magazine's 'Book of the Year' award. This was followed by *No Longer I?* comprising of stories and a study of Paul's words in Galatians 2:20.

Father of five children and six grandchildren, Howard now lives in retirement with Judy in Bournemouth.

Acknowledgements

I am indebted to two of my daughters: Naomi Willis for checking and correcting the grammar and punctuation of my poems, and Sarah Park for all her hard work in creating the wonderful illustrations that grace the book. I am grateful for all their suggestions and encouragement too.

I would also like to thank Luke and his team at Onwards and Upwards for their support, guidance, encouragement and patience in publishing this book.

Endorsements

Can anything new be said about Christmas? A dip into *Gift Beyond Measure* answers that question with a resounding yes. These poems, centred on the age-old story of the Nativity, abound in novel insights which warm the heart, amuse, inspire, and sometimes even startle. Thank you, Howard Webber, for giving us a new understanding of God's Christmas gift to the world.

John Larsson
General (Retired)
The Salvation Army

If you love Christmas, if you love the One who came to earth as a tiny baby and who will one day come again as King, and if you love the kind of verses that express profound truths in language that is – in the best sense of the word – simple, then you will love this book of poems by Howard Webber. For he too loves Christmas, he too loves the Lord of Christmas, and he has been gifted with the ability to write of these things in a winsome manner that will touch your heart and stay in your mind. I heartily recommend this collection of Howard's poems, and I think it will become a favourite that you will want to open again every year as the celebration of Christ's birth draws near

Chick Yuill
Writer, author, conference speaker, preacher,
Premier Christian Radio presenter

To my grandchildren:

Oscar
Amelie
Seth
Hettie
Rupert
Ray

Contents

Preface

Having been unable to find Christmas cards, even religious ones, that convey a clear message of what Christmas is about, I commenced writing pieces of poetry each year for the cards that I then created. Through the years many recipients of these cards have commented on the inspiration, encouragement and challenge the poems have been to them, adding that I ought to publish them together in a book.

Consequently this book, *Gift Beyond Measure*, was born. I have endeavoured to keep to what Matthew and Luke wrote in their Gospels, avoiding the many inaccuracies, myths and legends that have grown up around the Christmas story.

I hope that this little book will turn out to be a Gift Beyond Measure for you; something to accompany and edify you through the season of Advent, and a gift for friends and family, believers and non-believers, giving a timely reminder and clearer view of the great Gift Beyond Measure God gave us that first Christmas.

Broken

I crept up to the broken door
Of the broken cattle shed,
And just across the broken floor
Saw...
His broken manger-bed.

Even the silence was broken
By a baying, neighing sound;
Even the darkness was broken
As the lamplight shone around.

Even some tears had broken
Down his weary father's face;
Even her heart was broken
Giving birth in so foul a place.

Only one thing remained there,
Unblemished, unspoilt, undefiled;
Only one thing was unbroken,
That tiny, helpless child.

Yet this child would one day be broken,
Nailed to an old, broken tree;
And the one with the hammer and nails?
When I look, I am shocked, for it's me!

Christmas Wonder

See that star out in the darkness
Hanging over Bethlehem;
Has such tiny, gentle twinkling
Power far greater than the sun?

See that donkey lost in wonder
At the sight before its eyes?
Could this gift God offers man be
Known to ass yet not to wise?

See that baby in the stable,
Sucking at his mother's breast?
Can he be our God? – in nappies?
Choosing such a place to rest?

See that infant, soft and gentle,
Gurgling, burbling, full of joy.
Could the power that formed creation
Be contained within that boy?

See that love, so condescending,
Giving up his rightful throne.
How can I ignore his pleading,
'Let me make your heart my home'?

Hardly Noticed

Snow falls gently on the bandsmen
As they carol 'neath the lamp.
I stand somewhere in the shadows –
Hungry, tired, cold and damp.
Children, joyful, wave at Santa;
Eyes ablaze in Christmas light.
Shoppers' trolleys brimming over
As the band plays *Silent Night*.

By the band there stands a manger,
Dolly wrapped in sheets so white.
Parents sigh just like their children
At such undemanding sight.
Seeing me, expression changes:
Gone the smile, in place a glare.
Angry mummy stops Tom's staring;
Child, you recognised me there!

Carols finished, band departed;
They were busy, never saw
That the one so close beside them
Was the one they'd played them for.
Crowds rush by, lost in their bustling,
Like that night in Bethlehem.
Still they take no notice of me,
Still no room in hearts of men.

a gift so

bright &
beautiful

Christmas Gift

There is a gift more wonderful
Than any gift this world can give;
A gift so bright and beautiful
It makes our Christmas glitz seem drab.
Yet few have eyes to see that gift
Although they look into that stall;
And few reach out to grasp at it
Although they celebrate it all.

O Father, give us eyes to see
What lies beyond that tiny crib;
Beyond the babe in swaddling clothes,
Beyond the donkey, shepherds, shed.
Help us to see that which we miss,
Which would complete what isn't whole,
For underneath this Christmas wrap
Lies matchless bliss to swamp the soul.

Enjoy your family and your friends,
The carols, cards, the food, the fun.
Enjoy the children's shrieks of glee
As they delight in everything.
When then you take the tinsel down,
Return the tree to attic dark,
May you have found that gift sublime
And know him living in your heart.

Is This Our God?

Is this our God here, lying in a manger?
Did he forsake his palace and his throne?
Has he forgone the company of angels
To share the cattle's company and home?

And is our God, all-powerful and all-knowing,
Confined to flesh, with thoughts those of a babe?
And has the One who holds the world together
Entrusted his well-being to a maid?

Will not our God protect his own position,
Destroying all the men who wish him ill?
Or is it true he'll hang there limp and lifeless,
While letting men do to him what they will?

What caused our God to let this happen to him –
Humiliation, ridicule and pain?
How is it he considers us worth saving,
And bears all that and loves us just the same?

Christmas Joy – Christmas Lament

O Bethlehem! O Bethlehem!
How deaf and blind this world is to your message.
They've known it; they've seen it;
They've heard it all before.
The shepherds, the wise men,
The angels and the innkeeper –
Why can't men look beyond the words
And see there's so much more?

For an explosion of joy
Greets the one who hears the message,
Who seeks until he finds the Christ
As men did long ago.
For the brightness, peace and presence
They discovered in that manger,
Is the Christmas gift God offers still
To all who Christ would know.

So Bethlehem, dear Bethlehem,
Though deaf and blind the world is to your message,
Go shout it and show it
Like you've never done before.
You shepherds, you wise men, you angels at this
    Christmas time,
Pray for a world that needs to see
What you, in that manger, saw!

LOVE LONGS
to
ENTER EVERY
human heart

O Sweet Child

O vulnerable, sweet child,
Love of God, laid in a manger;
Gift-wrapped in straw inside a cattle shed.
Precious beyond the wealth of all earth's treasure,
Yet none will offer you their soft, clean bed.

O wonderful, sweet child,
Son of God, so condescending;
Reaching into our world so dead and dark.
Doors shut to you will not prevent you knocking;
Love longs to enter every human heart.

O beautiful, sweet child,
Prince of Peace, born into danger;
Worshipped by wise men in their finery.
More will reject than ever will adore you;
One day they'll even nail you to a tree.

Your Manger, Our Manger?

As I stand inside that stable in the darkness
And I gather up my coat to keep me warm,
My eyes pick out a baby in the lamplight –
A tiny little thing that's just been born.

It is hard to fully realise the marvel,
That the One who made the night sky's bright display,
The One whose wondrous presence filled the heavens,
Lies before me in a manger full of hay.

There within the manger lies the pure example
Of the path that all who follow him must share:
Not the high road, fame and greatness this world travels,
But the one that Love descends, but few men dare.

Teach us how to choose your lowly little shelter,
When so many would reject a cattle shed,
And when others seek their glory in a palace,
May we glory in your manger as our bed.

That Christmas

God came down in human form at Christmas.
He was just a tiny babe,
Who was cared for by a maid,
And was in a manger laid, that Christmas.

On the hills near Bethlehem, that Christmas,
In the stillness of the night
Angels came in radiance bright,
Woke the shepherds up in fright, that Christmas.

Listening to the angel's words, that Christmas,
They all set off with one mind,
Left their sleeping sheep behind,
Knowing not what they would find, that Christmas.

When they reached the cattle shed, that Christmas,
They were each one filled with awe
At the baby that they saw,
Sleeping in a bed of straw, that Christmas.

You can find him like they did, this Christmas.
For he left his heavenly throne
To make human hearts his home;
Seek him now, do not postpone, this Christmas.

this
GREATEST
OF GIFTS
seems so small

The Gift of Christmas

Lost in the holly and ivy;
Buried in cards wall to wall;
Immersed in a thousand sung carols
And smothered in tinsel and ball.
Deafened by the noise of the parties;
Entranced by a lit Christmas tree;
Blinded by the films on the tele;
Submerged in one great shopping spree.

Oft missed is that incalculable treasure,
That babe in the straw in a stall,
Devoid of all trappings and wrappings;
This greatest of gifts seems so small.
He seems such an unlikely answer
To the cries and the needs of mankind,
But the wise in this world who seek further,
Are then stunned, for it's God whom they find.

The Light on the Tree

No purple robe, just strips of cloth
Wrap round his precious little form,
Asleep within a cattle trough,
With only hay to keep him warm.

No palace grand for this young king,
His home is but a stable bare.
There isn't room in any inn
For he who will his heaven share.

No bulb-lit spruce or candled pine
Illumines this nativity.
Its brightness is God's Light Divine,
Who will himself hang on a tree.

So whilst you eat and dance and sing,
Remembering God's gift to you,
Do not forget his suffering,
For this was made for sharing too.

God's Whispered Word

What is it there within that shed
That brings men miles to bend their knee?
What is it hidden in the straw
That shepherds leave their flocks to see,
When local folks who live nearby
Pass by the place indifferently?

God's whispered Word to those with ears;
His still small voice is in that stall.
God's candlelight's in Bethlehem,
A flickering thing, so pure, so small,
That only those with eyes to see
Perceive his secret in it all.

Lord, place your Word within my heart,
And make my soul your manger bed,
That whether noticed or ignored
My life may speak what your life said:
That those who have the eyes to see
May meet you in this cattle shed.

A CANDLE
glimmering

IN THE DARK

Christmas – Heaven Come Down

A far-off dream, a distant hope;
A sparkle, light years off, remote.
A candle glimmering in the dark,
Beyond our reach, elusive, stark.

Angels have wings with which to soar
Those heights we can but hanker for.
We have no means to bring heaven low,
To scan its incandescent glow.

Yet mercy constrained that glorious Light
To bring His day into our night.
Yes, heaven came down in one small babe,
Who in a cattle trough was laid.

Few were awake, few saw that dawn,
Few saw beyond that tiny form.
And still today few wake and see
What God still offers you and me.

If Only

I wish I'd known what I know now,
I could have known it then.
For I was there when he was born,
I lived in Bethlehem.

I'd heard of an unmarried girl,
Arriving nine months gone,
And how there was no room for her
To have her little one.

I'd heard she had a little boy,
And laid him in a trough.
I wish now that I'd offered help,
I'd heard they weren't well off.

But like so many in that town,
I kept myself away
Except to moan about the noise
When shepherds came one day.

If only I had realised
Who lay there in that shed,
I would have opened up my home
And given him my bed.

The School Nativity

Boys in dressing gowns surround the manger;
Dolly wrapped in tea towel in the straw;
Girl with plastic wings
Picks her nose and loudly sings
As a wise man drops his myrrh upon the floor.

The village crowd into this school performance;
Parents smile whilst teachers start to flap,
As dear Mary fails to say
Lines she's practised every day,
And her brother shouts, to prompt her, from the back.

We find these school nativities amusing,
The things they do, the way they get things wrong.
Yet what we fail to see
Is the script for you and me
That's been waiting our attention for so long.

So when your splitting sides are sore with laughter,
Recovering, while they sing *Silent Night*,
Remember, in the hay
Lies the One who wrote our play,
Who is waiting, still, for us to get it right!

FOR
THOSE WHO
want enough

God's Secret Stair

No Dorchester or palace grand;
No five star en suite room.
No carpet red with entourage;
No paparazzi zoom.
No flash bulbs, questions, razzmatazz;
No banquets, cavalcades.
No television interviews –
No hype or masquerade.

But down a quiet, secret stair
God chose to send his Son –
The greatest drama to unfold
Since history begun.
God crept into the world, a babe.
Dependent on a girl
For love, for life, for sustenance,
Was he who made the world.

Yet hidden in that helpless thing,
That baby in a trough,
Is life and hope beyond the dreams
For those who want enough.
For those who see beyond their eyes,
That baby is the key
To one unending Christmas
God offers you and me.

A Shepherd's Story

The night is quiet, cold and dark;
The chill wind whistles through the trees.
Wrapped up in woollen blanket tight,
Protected from the winter breeze,
I watch my sheep enfold their lambs
As they relax and rest at ease.

Quite suddenly the sky lights up
As though a star has landed, then
A man appears whose thunderous voice
Tells of a birth in Bethlehem.
More angels now fill up the sky
Bringing us sight and sound of heaven.

We leave our flocks and head for town,
Doing as the angel said,
And find the parents and the child
Lodging in a cattle shed.
I gaze intensely at the babe,
But catch a glimpse of God instead.

What a Gift

On a night, dark and cold,
Came a gift, long foretold,
Far more precious than gold,
Who'd grow up to be bold
And to break Satan's hold,
And bring blessings untold.

And the angels?   They praised
The shepherds?   All gazed.
The parents?   Both dazed.
The wise men?   Amazed.
King Herod?   Half-crazed.
And Bethlehem?   Just lazed.

By the life that he led,
And the words that he said,
And the food that he fed,
And the blood that he shed
When he died in our stead,
He still raises the dead
…if we let him.

wonder AT THE Sight

Angels Singing

Angels singing songs of praises
In the dead of night.
Shepherds, out in lonely places,
Wonder at the sight.
Told to go and seek a baby;
They obey and find the Light.

Rich, wise men are looking skywards,
See a sparkling gem.
Follow as it leads them westwards
And to Bethlehem.
There they find within a cowshed
One whose greatness humbles them.

How I wish that, like the shepherds,
I could angels see;
Or that star, that God sent wise men,
He would send to me.
O to see that little baby,
There, at his nativity.

Truth is, God to every person
Sends a heavenly ray,
Which would lead them all to Jesus
In the self-same way.
They'd discover God's best treasure
In that manger wrapped in hay.

Christmas Day

A couple came to Bethlehem
With nowhere else to stay;
They took a humble cattle shed
In time for Christmas Day.

Their child was born within that place,
Half-hidden in the hay;
His cot, the cattle's eating trough,
On that first Christmas Day.

Some shepherds came in from the cold
To where the baby lay,
And knelt before the One whose birth
Created Christmas Day.

Years later, with expensive gifts,
Wise men did homage pay,
And found 'twas not their gifts, but he
Who makes their Christmas Day.

You wish that Christmas time could last?
You wish that it could stay?
Then seek the only One who can
Make each day Christmas Day.

I Have Heard

I have heard of hosts of angels
Hovering above the earth,
Heralding Christ Jesus' coming,
Telling shepherds of his birth.

In response, I'm told, the shepherds
Went in search to Bethlehem;
Found the Christ-child in a manger;
Left his presence different men.

Later, so they say, came wise men
Bringing treasures rich and rare;
They bowed down in sheer amazement
When they found the Saviour there.

Have I ever seen an angel?
Can I prove the stories true?
Why do I believe these stories?
Why? Because I've found him too!

THAT

GOD

himself
should do

ALL THAT

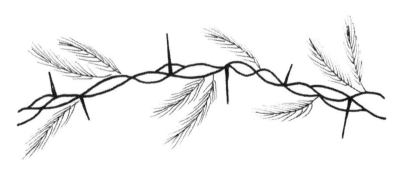

Incredible!

Incredible! Incredulous! Impossible! Unknown?
A child born to a virgin?
Yet God has clearly shown
How poor our wealth of knowledge is
When measured by his own.

No man could have imagined
Or thought up such a plan,
To save this sinful, fallen world
And offer hope to man.
No good we do can ever do
What God in Jesus can.

In Christ, God came in human form
And did himself abase,
Revealing his enormous love
By dying in our place,
That now we might be right with him
And one day see his face.

Incredible! Incredulous! Impossible! But true!
That God himself should do all that
For love of me and you.
Go check it out; seek him yourself,
As wise men did and do.

The Baby

I'm elated at seeing this beautiful baby,
This bubbly, gurgling bundle of joy.
Amazed at the grip that he has on my heartstrings,
My soul's deeply stirred at the sight of this boy.

What a gift is this child God has sent us from heaven;
What a risk he has taken to send us his Son;
What a start, to be laid in some hay in a manger;
What on earth will become of this dear little one?

Lamb of God

O Lamb of God, in a stable born,
Shepherds go seeking to find you,
But when they do, they have yet to know
That you will their "Shepherd" be.

In Bethlehem (known as House of Bread),
Laid in a trough meant for feeding,
Will they discover The Bread of Life,
The food that their souls long for?

Wise men or kings bring great gifts to you;
God's Wisdom, clothed in a toddler.
Do they behold just an earthly king,
Or someone sublime from heaven?

Come now, bow down, let us worship him,
As both our King and our Saviour;
Feed on the food that he offers us,
And make him our Shepherd too.

A
gift so
Wonderful,
Sublime

Christmas Mystery

Here, snuggled in a feeding trough
God offers us a mystery:
A gift so wonderful, sublime,
Though many look, most fail to see.

The shepherds come, yet do they know
That he will their Good Shepherd be?
That he'll replace their Temple lambs?
God's sacrificial Lamb is he.

The wise men bow before the child
Whose wisdom outweighs theirs by far.
Do they not know that it was he
Who put in place their guiding star?

Here lies much more than meets the eye,
A sight that only hearts can see;
As Christmas comes, God tries again
To show his heart to you and me.

But Made Himself Nothing[1]

It is hard to conceive or imagine
How God could have done what he did,
When he came in the form of a human
And chose on this planet to live.

Though present throughout the whole cosmos,
He made himself ever so small:
Just a cell in the womb of a woman,
Then a babe in a trough in a stall.

Though he formed both the earth and the heavens,
And all power and knowledge were his,
He now lies there so tiny and helpless,
Dependent on two teenage kids!

Though he came willing, knowing his future,
As a man he will learn it anew
And accept, as he did when in heaven,
What awaits him to save me and you.

---

[1] Philippians 2:7

Joseph's Story

'Pregnant, Mary? How can that be?
When did you ever sleep with me?
I trusted you. We'll have to part.
You broke your vow and broke my heart.

'I thought you pure. I loved you so.
What shall I do? I just don't know.
Why lie and say, "An angel came,"
To make believe you're not to blame?

'O Mary, still I love you so,
And I don't want the world to know
How you have caused me so much pain,
Nor do I wish to spoil your name.'

'Joseph, what she says is true
And what she heard, I now tell you,
For Mary is God's chosen one;
The child she carries? God's own Son!'

NO
Joy
COMPARES
WITH WHAT
he will bring

It's Christmas Time

It's Christmas time, rejoice and sing,
Bring praises to our God and King,
Who left his throne in heaven to bring
Us mortal men salvation.

He came right down from heaven to earth
To offer all a second birth,
A second chance, a sense of great worth,
A wonderful salvation.

He came to die upon a cross,
And for our gain he suffered loss.
He gave us "gold" and took all our dross,
That we might know salvation.

He died to take away our sin,
To show us what we mean to him.
No joy compares with what he will bring
To all who seek his salvation.

Why?

Why do you fall upon your knees
As you enter this cattle shed?
Is it because of the heavenly host
And the words that the angel said?
Or is it because of something sublime
That you see in that old manger bed?

Why do you fall upon your knees
At the sight of this toddler at play?
Is it because of the star in the sky
Which led you to travel this way?
Or is it because you've glimpsed the divine
In the child, that such homage you pay?

Why do you fall upon your knees
When you view the Nativity?
Is it because your emotions are stirred
At the heart-warming scene that you see?
Or is it because, beyond sight and sound,
You've discovered the reality?

Like Any Other Child?

Jesus grew in Mary's womb
Like any other child.
He was born that Christmas morn
Like any other child.
Weak and helpless, prone to cry
Like any other child.
Yet this little one was not
Like any other child.

Nestled in his mother's arms
Like any other child.
Thirsty for his mother's milk
Like any other child.
Needing her protective love
Like any other child.
Yet life would prove he was not
Like any other child.

He would die upon a cross
Like no other man.
Take the blame for all of us
Like no other man.
Come alive and conquer death
Like no other man.
Dwell within all who believe
Like no other man.

TURN YOUR
DARKNESS
INTO
light

Darkness into Light

Cold and frosty, dark and gloomy,
Was that winter world back then.
Joy and hope had long been absent;
Tyranny had crushed most men.

Then God spoke into the darkness
In the most unlikely way;
Placed his Light within a manger,
Light to turn men's night to day.

And that Light would grow in splendour,
Bringing peace in place of fears,
Giving hope and help to many;
Healing wounds and drying tears.

If your life is dark and gloomy,
Bleaker than a winter's night,
Seek the One who longs to change it,
Turn your darkness into light.

I Never Knew

I never knew what sunshine was
Till I looked into his face.
I never knew what heaven was
Till I stepped into that place.

This Prince was wrapped in torn-up rags
With a manger for his cot;
His palace was a cattle shed;
Rich and famous he was not.

Yet I instinctively bowed low;
When I saw him I just knew,
God had sent his promised Saviour
Down this humble avenue.

Shepherd of Shepherds

Shepherd of shepherds, King of all kings,
Great God Creator of all living things.
Now in a manger, confined in a babe,
Limited, just like the creatures he made.

One day he'll die and be nailed to a cross,
He'll offer his gold in exchange for our dross.
Yet, death will not hold this incredible man,
For he will arise and destroy Satan's plan.

On clouds he'll ascend to his heavenly home,
And regain his majesty, power and throne.
And then he'll return in his glory to bring
To heaven, forever, all those who love him.

So celebrate Christmas with carols and cards
And turkey and crackers and games of charades,
But find quiet moments to ponder, review,
And think about Jesus, Jesus and you.

Joy
&
laughter
fill the air

Who Is He?

Who is he laid in a manger,
In that dark, dank, dismal place?
Is he really God's great answer
To our sin, shame and disgrace?

Who would give away their baby
If they really loved their child,
Knowing how their child would suffer,
How their gift would be defiled?

Who can understand God's mercy,
Comprehend what he has done,
Loving such unworthy creatures,
Giving us his precious Son?

Trees aglow with lights at Christmas,
Joy and laughter fill the air.
But another tree is waiting,
They will hang that baby there.

How Can It Be?

How can it be
That he who made the world and every galaxy,
Could come to earth revealing such humility?
How can it be?

How can it be
That leaving all his glory and his majesty,
His heavenly home, his power and his enormity,
He chose the limitations of humanity,
Exchanging all his riches for our poverty?
How can it be?

How can it be
That one day he would choose such ghastly agony?
And bear the taunts, the blows and nails unflinchingly,
Because he longed for our eternal company?
And that he did it all for such a one as me?
How can it be?

Reveal to Me

As I observe that manger bed
And glimpse that little sleepy head,
Reveal to me the heart of love
That sent my Saviour from above.

Before he came you knew the cost,
That man would nail him to a cross.
Yet, still you gave in faith that some
Would recognise and love your Son.

Though so much can swamp Christmas time,
Like shopping, parties, pantomime,
And even church activity,
Lord, show afresh your gift to me.

BRINGING

peace & joy

TO MEN

Christ is Born in Bethlehem

Christ is born in Bethlehem,
Bringing peace and joy to men.
Why not let the Christ-child bring
That peace and joy to you?

Angels celebrate his birth,
Shepherds leave their sheep to search.
Why delay discovering
The One who's seeking you?

Magi travel far to see,
In a manger, Majesty!
Why hold back from seeking him
When you could find him too?

This, God's Son, will one day die
On a cross of wood, hung high.
Why ignore his suffering?
He did it all for you!

The Magi

As we surveyed the starlit skies,
It took us weeks to realise,
The twinkling new celestial thing
Was heralding a new-born king.

The "star" was moving westerly;
It seemed to beckon, 'Follow me!'
And so began an episode
Upon a long and dangerous road.

When we arrived, eventually,
We each were so surprised to see
No palace grand, no guard of men;
A humble home in Bethlehem.

As we then stooped inside we saw
A toddler playing on the floor.
We knew, instinctively, that he
Was who we'd come so far to see.

'Gold, frankincense and myrrh we bring
To lay before your feet, O king.'
He stopped and looked most knowingly,
As we each bowed on bended knee.

I never will forget that boy,
I wonder, was his life all joy?
And did he one day wear a crown,
Sit on his throne in purple gown?

The only thing I ever heard
(And I dismissed it as absurd)
Was that he died in agony;
That men had nailed him to a tree.

never assume

where it is

HE WILL
GUIDE

Guiding Light

Men searched and found the sign God sent before them.
They left their all to go just where he led,
But from its guiding light their eyes were lowered
To seek their guidance from mere men instead.

Yet, though they turned and sought an earthly answer –
Sight of a palace grand had turned their head –
God waited patiently for them to follow,
And find the Christ-child in a humble shed.

Star in the firmament, Light in the darkness,
Follow that finger of God in the sky.
Trust in the Lord, not one's own understanding,
Never assume where it is he will guide.
If you anticipate: "Prince... in a palace!"
You may well miss what he longs to confide.

When I Was Young

Like many a child, when I was young
I woke before the birds had sung,
And there across the room I saw
My sack, now full, upon the floor.

Excitedly, I soon unwrapped
The contents of the bulging sack,
And found in each a new surprise
That brought delight to sleepy eyes.

Inside my window frost had formed;
I breathed on it, and as it warmed
A hole appeared; I looked to see
If Santa would wave back to me.

There was no Santa in the sky,
I saw no sleigh or reindeer fly;
Though Mum called out, 'Go back to bed,'
I played with my new toys instead.

Next Christmas I awoke to noise;
I saw my dad bring in my toys,
Destroying childhood fantasy
Of Santa's generosity.

Some think that the Nativity,
Like Santa, is absurdity;
Though it may seem far-fetched, it's true:
Christ came, a babe, for me and you.

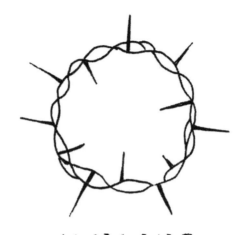

MAY HIS
Peace
AND
Goodwill

REIGN

Let Us Celebrate

Let us celebrate the coming
Of the baby born a King;
Join with shepherds, wise men, angels,
Come just now and worship him.

God so loved the world he gave us
Jesus Christ, his only Son,
So that we might live forever
And together be as one.

As a tiny little baby
He came down from heaven to earth;
Chose a girl, so young and humble,
And a stable for his birth.

Never was there one more lovely,
Yet, he would rejected be,
And would suffer, even dying,
Out of love for you and me.

As we celebrate Christ's coming,
May his peace and goodwill reign
In the hearts of all the people
Who profess and own his name.

God's Love Story

Many were the years that men had waited –
Watching, hoping, praying for an end
To the shame and unrelenting darkness,
And the conquering Saviour God would send.

But God's answer was most unexpected,
For he came as gentle as a dove,
Not to conquer with a mighty army,
But to show a heart brimful with love.

God came down himself, a tiny baby,
Made a cattle feeding trough his bed.
Leaving heaven's glory and security,
Choosing vulnerability instead.

Poor and rich both knelt in adoration,
Though hatred was never far away;
It would grow despite his faultless goodness,
And would nail him to a tree one day.

Yet the grave could not end God's love story,
For Christ Jesus, now with wounds, returned,
Reaching out with love to those who'd failed him,
And through cowardice his way had spurned.

As we look upon your gift at Christmas,
Lying in the straw, dear Lord, we pray:
Help us live to show to you our gratitude
For the sacrifice that your Love made.

A GIFT FAR MORE PRECIOUS THAN GOLD

Finding Jesus

The sky was so filled with the angels,
Each heralding God's gift of love,
It transfixed the shepherds below them
At seeing God's glory above.

The heavenly host then departed,
The shepherds to Bethlehem went
To find what an angel had told them:
The gift that the Father had sent.

They found, in some straw in a manger,
The One that the prophets foretold:
God's answer to man's deepest longing;
A gift far more precious than gold.

On leaving they couldn't keep silent
About what they'd heard and they'd seen,
Amazing the people who met them
With what must have felt like a dream.

And you? If you seek him you'll find him
And struggle to keep silent too.
You'll long to tell others of Jesus
And what meeting him did for you.

Consequences

Travelling home from Bethlehem,
I'm sure they never knew
The seed that they had planted
And the damage it would do.

How troops would enter every home
Around and in that town,
And butcher all the baby boys
To save King Herod's crown.

If only they had kept their eyes
Upon God's heavenly sign,
King Herod may have never known
Or carried out that crime.

But when the Magi told him of
A new king born nearby,
Alarmed, he had to find the child;
The infant had to die.

Forewarned, the One he sought to kill
Escaped before troops came
And slaughtered all the innocents
In wicked Herod's name.

The wisest men are foolish still
When they, like you and I,
Replace God-given guidance and
On other things rely.

We may correct the error made,
And things work out just so,
But what of consequences that
We never ever know?

So teach me how to trust in you
To always be my guide,
And when I'm pulled another way,
Lord, keep me by your side.

GOD gave his ALL

Gift Beyond Measure

Gift beyond measure,
Gift beyond price;
Unequalled treasure,
God's sacrifice.
Exchanging his glorious heavenly home,
A shed now his palace, a trough now his throne.

Babe in a manger,
Babe, oh so small;
Embracing danger,
God gave his all.
Improbable start to a wonderful plan
Whereby God could rescue condemned, fallen man.

Hope of the ages,
Hope of today;
Foretold by sages,
There in the hay.
Transforming the life of the seeker who'll find
That Jesus is real and alive and divine.

When Jesus Comes Again

The day is drawing ever near
When Christ will come, will reappear;
No virgin birth, no manger bed,
No shepherds, magi, cattle shed.

But from above the clouds, the skies,
He'll come as King with fiery eyes;
His face as radiant as the sun,
A splendour seen by everyone.

Yes, he who hammered in each nail
And did Christ's hands and feet impale,
Together with the baying crowd
Who shouted 'Crucify!' out loud.

Those Pharisees and Pilate too,
And all who claim they never knew,
Will kneel and weep at seeing him,
The Crucified, return as King.

With tears of joy and bended knee,
Those praying, labouring ceaselessly,
Will worship, praise, rejoice, adore,
The One so long they've waited for.

So be prepared for that great day,
When death, pain, tears, he'll wipe away,
And faithful souls he'll gather in
To spend eternity with him.

THE GIFT OF

Christmas

Also by Howard Webber

Meeting Jesus

Publisher: Shield Books
ISBN: 978-0-85412-823-5

How the power of the gospel of Jesus Christ can work in the lives of ordinary men and women – the sort you might meet at a garden gate, or in a pub, on a bench by a church wall near a car park. This book isn't about overwhelming success – but it is about the reality of what happens when people meet Jesus and about the kind of change he can affect when given the space to do his work.

"It is all too easy to see the role of being God's ambassadors as reduced to preaching, or set among those who we love and are safe. But this book challenges us to be where Jesus would be, with the down-and-outs, with the hopeless and the broken. It looks the cost of such ministry square in the eye and carries on just the same. Please buy this book." – Christianity Magazine

No Longer I?

Publisher: Gracednotes Ministries
ISBN: 9781519451804

Don't allow the negativity of some within the Body to determine your own walk with The Lord. Often, when we long to do what is pleasing to God, it seems that there are insurmountable problems and difficulties that Satan throws at us in all sorts of subtle ways. Webber provides an open account of how he came to understand that the discouragements and hurts we suffer from fellow believers, together with our feelings of inadequacy, are no barrier to God and what he can do.

"...an examination of what it means to really surrender to God, put yourself to one side and work simply for his glory." – **Premier Christianity**

Similar Books from the Publisher

The Shepherd Spy
Angie McEvansoneya
ISBN 978-1-78815-677-6

12 nativity plays for children of all ages and for groups of all sizes. Each play presents a different slant on the Christmas story, with the author's licence as to some of the surrounding details. We look at the nativity through different eyes – those of mice, a young spy of Herod's, the national news channel, the stars and others.

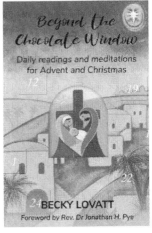

Beyond the Chocolate Window
Becky Lovatt
ISBN 978-1-78815-633-2

Daily meditations for Advent and Christmas, offering new insights into well-known stories. Becky Lovatt invites us to join her on a journey through the Bible, exploring the thoughts and feelings of some of the people touched by God, so that we too can deepen our relationship with him.

Books available from all good bookshops and from the publisher: **www.onwardsandupwards.org/shop**